Dollar Diplomacy

Jackson Cooper

Copyright Page

Index

Jackson Cooper

What Are Taxes and Why Do We Pay Them?

Taxes are part of our daily lives, even if we often don't realize it. Every time you buy something at a store, fill up your gas tank, or even collect your paycheck, you are contributing a portion of your money to the system that keeps a country running. But why do we have to pay taxes? Is it just a whim of the government, or is there a deeper reason behind all of this? Imagine for a moment a world without paved streets, public schools, accessible hospitals, or police officers protecting our cities. Taxes are the engine that allows all of these things to exist.

When we pay taxes, we are essentially funding the services that we all use, whether we want to or not. From the street lights that illuminate our streets at night to the firefighters who respond to an emergency, those services cost money, and taxes are how those costs are covered. We may not always see it right away, but every penny we pay has a purpose, even if we don't always agree with how it is spent. In other words, taxes are not just an obligation, they are a way to contribute to the well-being of the community in which we live.

The problem for many people, however, is that they don't feel like they're getting a fair value for what they pay. Maybe you've felt like the money taken out of your paycheck could be better spent in your own pocket, being used for your own needs. That's a valid concern, and it's normal to wonder if those funds are really being put to the best use. But the truth is, without that income, things we take for granted, like public education, transportation, or safety, would be impossible to maintain. So, while we may not always like it, taxes are a necessary evil for society to function.

At the same time, there is an element of responsibility in paying taxes. We live in a world where it is easy to fall into the trap of thinking that "if I don't pay, nothing happens." But if every person decides not to fulfill this responsibility, the entire system would collapse. That is why paying taxes is not only a legal issue, it is a matter of principle. It is a way of contributing to collective progress, of ensuring that future generations have access to the same or even better opportunities that we had.

Of course, not everything is perfect. We know that tax systems can be complicated, unfair, or even abusive in some cases. But understanding how they work is the first step to being able to manage them better. Because, although taxes may seem like a burden, they are also a powerful tool that we can learn to use to our advantage. The key is to educate ourselves, to know our obligations and rights, and to take advantage of the legal opportunities that exist to reduce what we pay without falling into incorrect or risky practices.

In this world, we are all connected. When we pay taxes, we are not only helping ourselves, but also our neighbors, friends, and family. It is an act of solidarity, even if we don't always see it that way. At the end of the day, taxes are an investment in where we live, in the future of our community, and in the quality of life for everyone. It's easy to feel like we're losing money, but if you think about it, what we're really doing is building a bridge to a safer and more stable tomorrow. And that's a price that, even if it costs us, is worth paying.

The Tax System Exposed

The tax system is like an invisible web that connects all citizens to the government. Although it often seems complicated and overwhelming, it actually boils down to one basic idea: people and businesses generate income, and a portion of that money is used to fund services and projects that benefit society. The problem is that this invisible web is not always easily understood, and what should be a clear process can feel like a game with hidden rules. That's why knowing how the tax system works is key to making better decisions with your money and avoiding costly mistakes.

First, it's important to know that the tax system is organized around different types of taxes. There are direct taxes, like income tax, that apply directly to what you earn. Then there are indirect taxes, like consumption taxes, that you pay when you buy goods or services. There are also specific taxes, like property taxes, that depend on what you own, whether it's a house, a car, or even shares in a company. Each of these taxes has a specific purpose and a set of rules that govern them. And while they sometimes feel like a burden, they are designed to spread the cost of running the government across everyone.

The heart of the tax system is income tax, which is probably the one you feel the most on a day-to-day basis. This tax is based on your income, and the more you make, the more you pay, at least in theory. The key here is to understand that not all of the money you make is taxable. There are deductions, exemptions, and tax credits that can reduce the amount of income that is actually considered taxable. For example, if you pay interest on a mortgage or have significant medical expenses, you could use those figures to lower what you have to pay at the end of the year. This is a point where many people miss opportunities because they don't understand how to take advantage of these legal tools.

Then there are consumption taxes, such as VAT or taxes on specific goods, such as alcohol or gasoline. These taxes don't depend on how much you earn, but on how much you spend and what you spend it on. The interesting thing about consumption taxes is that they affect everyone equally, regardless of their income, because every time you buy something, you're contributing to the system. Although they may seem less visible, at the end of the day they represent a significant part of what the government collects. And this is where personal planning comes into play: knowing how you spend your money can help you minimize the impact of these taxes on your budget.

On the other hand, there are property and estate taxes. If you own a home, you are probably familiar with property taxes. These types of taxes are essential to funding local services, such as trash collection, park maintenance, and public safety. Although it is not always obvious, what you pay in these types of taxes has a direct impact on the quality of services you receive in your community. That is why it is important to know how this tax is calculated and what options you have to reduce it if possible.

The tax system also includes taxes on specific activities, such as business or investments. If you own a business, the tax system can seem especially intimidating. There are taxes on sales, on profits, and in some cases, on the goods you import or export. But at the same time, business owners have access to a wide variety of tax deductions that can significantly reduce what they have to pay. This means that if you understand the rules, you can turn the tax system into a friend rather than a hindrance.

Now, what makes the tax system complex isn't the taxes themselves, but the rules and exceptions that come with them. Every country has its own tax laws, and within each country, there may be different laws at the state, regional, or local level. This can make even the most organized people feel like they're never completely up to date with their tax obligations. There's one thing to remember, though: the tax system isn't designed to trap you—it's designed to collect money efficiently. If you take the time to learn how it works and seek advice when you need it, you can navigate it successfully.

Ultimately, the tax system is a powerful tool that affects everyone, but also offers opportunities for those who know how to navigate it. It's not just about paying what you owe, but about understanding how you can optimize your income and expenses to make the most of the rules that exist. In the end, the goal is not just to meet your obligations, but to do so intelligently, so that you can build a stronger financial life while contributing to the well-being of the society in which you live. With a little knowledge and planning, the tax system can stop being an enemy and become a useful tool for your future.

The Tax Return Without Mysteries

Filing your taxes can feel like a daunting task, filled with technical terms and endless forms. Many people get stressed out just thinking about it, but the truth is that it doesn't have to be that complicated. A tax return is simply a report you give to the government to show how much you earned in the year, how much you've already paid in taxes, and whether you're owed more or get a refund. It's like making a financial summary of your life over the past year, and while it may seem tedious, it's essential to keeping your finances in order and avoiding problems in the future.

The first step to taking the mystery out of filing taxes is knowing what information you need. It all starts with your income. If you're an employee, you probably receive an annual document from your company detailing how much you earned and how much was withheld in taxes. If you're self-employed, you'll likely need to gather invoices, receipts, and any other records that show how much money you made. You also need to have information on hand about your expenses, especially if some of them may be deductible. This includes things like medical expenses, mortgage interest, donations to charities, and even expenses related to your job or business.

One of the most common mistakes when filing taxes is not knowing what you can deduct. This is where many people lose money. A tax deduction reduces the amount of your income that is subject to taxes, meaning you could pay less. For example, if you had significant medical expenses, you may be able to use them to reduce your taxable income. The same goes if you paid for courses or training related to your job. The secret is to know the rules and make sure you keep all the necessary records. You never know when the government might ask for proof.

Another key point is to understand the difference between tax credits and deductions. While deductions reduce your taxable income, tax credits are even more powerful because they are subtracted directly from the amount of tax you owe. For example, if you owe $1,000 in taxes and you have a $200 tax credit, you'll only pay $800. Some credits are refundable, meaning that even if you don't owe anything in taxes, you could still get money back. Researching what tax credits are available for your situation can save you a significant amount of money.

Once you have all your information ready, the next step is to choose how to file your return. Today, there are several options. You can do it yourself using specialized software, hire an accountant, or even file manually in some cases. The advantage of software programs is that they are usually easy to use and designed to guide you step by step. On the other hand, an accountant can be a big help if your finances are more complicated, such as when you have multiple sources of income, your own business, or complex investments. While hiring a professional can cost money, the savings you achieve thanks to their expertise often offsets that expense.

One thing many people forget is to proofread their return before they send it in. Making mistakes can be costly, either by overpaying or by having the government ask for corrections, which can lead to penalties or interest. Make sure all the numbers are correct, that you've included all the necessary information, and that you haven't forgotten any credits or deductions you can claim. Take your time doing this final check, because it's better to get it right the first time than to have to correct it later.

Another important issue is knowing what to do if you cannot pay the taxes you owe. Many people panic when they realize that the amount they owe is higher than they expected, but there are solutions. Most governments offer installment payment options or financing plans so you can settle your debt without breaking the bank. The most important thing is not to ignore the problem. Contacting the tax authorities and reaching an agreement is always a better option than letting the debt grow with interest and penalties.

Last but not least, keep all documentation related to your tax return. Although it may seem unnecessary, it is crucial to have a record of everything you filed in case you ever need to justify it. Generally, it is recommended to keep these documents for at least five years, but this can vary depending on the laws of your country. Having an organized file with all your tax information can save you a lot of headaches in the future.

Filing taxes doesn't have to be a mystery or an insurmountable burden. It's simply one part of the system that allows us to live in an organized, public-service society. Understanding how it works, what you need, and what your rights are can transform a seemingly daunting task into something much more manageable. And best of all, by doing things right, you can take advantage of legal opportunities to reduce your tax burden and maximize your income. At the end of the day, it's all about taking control of your finances and using the tax system to your advantage.

Your Best Ally

When you hear the word "taxes," you probably think of a burden, a cost, or even something you'd rather avoid at all costs. But what if I told you that the tax system could become your best ally? It may sound strange, almost contradictory, but understanding how taxes work and learning how to use them to your advantage can completely change the way you view your finances. The trick is to stop seeing them as an enemy and start considering them as a tool that, if you know how to use it, can help you achieve your financial goals.

The first step to turning taxes into an ally is to change your mindset. Many people view taxes as nothing more than money that goes away and never comes back. But the truth is that the tax system is full of opportunities if you know where to look. There are deductions, credits, benefits, and strategies designed for individuals and businesses who understand how to take advantage of them. If you're willing to invest some time and effort into educating yourself, you'll soon realize that you can reduce what you pay while still taking advantage of the rules in place.

One of the most effective ways to make the tax system work for you is through planning. It's not just about filing your return once a year and then forgetting about it. The real key is planning throughout the year. For example, if you know that some expenses are deductible, you can make smarter decisions about how and when you spend. If you're thinking about making a donation to a cause you care about, doing so before the tax year ends could help reduce your tax burden. The same goes for investing in your education or business improvements. Planning ahead allows you to take advantage of every opportunity and minimize the impact of taxes on your pocketbook.

Another important aspect is knowing what tax deductions and credits apply to your situation. For example, many people don't know that medical expenses can be deductible in certain cases, or that investing in renewable energy for your home could give you access to tax credits. If you own a business, the possibilities are even greater. From office expenses to technology investments, the tax system is designed to support those who create jobs and contribute to the economy. The key is knowing what benefits are available and making sure you qualify to take advantage of them.

If you own a business, the tax system can be your best ally in growing and expanding. For example, expenses related to the operation of your business, such as rent, supplies, equipment, and even some travel, can be deductible. This means that you are not only investing in the growth of your company, but you are also reducing the amount of taxable income. Additionally, many jurisdictions offer specific tax incentives for certain sectors, such as technology or agriculture. Researching what programs exist in your area can open doors that you didn't even know were there.

Saving for retirement is another perfect example of how taxes can work in your favor. In many countries, contributions to retirement savings accounts are tax-deductible, meaning you can reduce your taxable income while securing your financial future. Plus, some governments offer additional incentives, such as matching a portion of your contributions. Not only is this a smart way to save, but it's also an effective way to reduce what you pay in taxes today.

One tool that is often overlooked is tax breaks. If you have dependents, such as children or elderly parents, you may qualify for breaks that significantly reduce your taxable income. These breaks are designed to ease the burden on those with additional responsibilities, and not taking advantage of them would be like leaving money on the table. Make sure you include all relevant details when filing to maximize the benefits you can reap.

Of course, you don't have to do it all alone. Working with a professional, such as an accountant or tax advisor, can make a big difference. These experts are trained to identify opportunities that may not be obvious to you and can help you build a tax strategy that fits your specific needs. While hiring a professional may seem like an added expense, it often translates into much bigger savings in the long run. A good advisor will not only help you meet your legal obligations, but will also teach you how to use the tax system to your advantage.

Finally, remember that knowledge is power. The more you know about how the tax system works, the better equipped you will be to make smart decisions. You don't need to become an expert, but it is important to understand the basics and stay on top of changes in tax laws. Even small adjustments, like saving receipts or taking advantage of a deduction you didn't know about, can have a significant impact on your personal finances.

Taxes don't have to be an enemy. On the contrary, they can be a powerful tool to help you build a more stable and successful financial life. It all starts with a change of perspective and a commitment to learning how to take advantage of the opportunities within your reach. When you do that, you stop feeling like the tax system is against you and start seeing it as an ally that propels you toward your goals. Because at the end of the day, it's not about how much you make, it's about how you use what you have to create a better future.

Extra Money in Your Pocket

Who doesn't want a little extra money in their pocket? It's an appealing idea, but for many it seems like a distant dream. What few people realize, however, is that the tax system, with all its rules and exceptions, can be a powerful tool to help you keep more of your money. It's not about magic or finding illegal shortcuts; it's about knowing your rights, taking advantage of the opportunities the system offers you, and, in essence, playing smart by the rules of the game.

One of the most effective ways to put extra money in your pocket is to be well-versed in the tax deductions you can claim on your tax return. For example, if you have a regular job and spend money on transportation, uniforms, or tools necessary to perform your job, you may be able to deduct those costs. If you work from home, you may even be able to deduct a portion of your utilities, like electricity and internet, as long as you have a designated space exclusively for working. While it may seem insignificant, all of these small deductions add up, and at the end of the year you might be surprised by how much you managed to save.

Another aspect that many people overlook is the potential for tax credits. While deductions reduce your taxable income, tax credits are even more valuable because they directly reduce the amount of tax you have to pay. Some credits are specifically designed for certain groups, such as parents, students, or people who invest in renewable energy. For example, if you have children, you might qualify for a credit for each of them, which could mean significant relief on your tax bill. Researching available credits and making sure you qualify can make the difference between getting a refund or having to pay.

If you're a business owner, you have even more opportunities to put extra money in your pocket. Many times, expenses related to your business are deductible. This includes things like your office rent, the wages you pay your employees, the equipment you purchase, and even some business travel. But here's the catch: You need to keep detailed, organized records of all of your expenses. It's not enough to just know that you can deduct something; you need receipts, invoices, and any other documents that support your claims. Organization is key to making sure you take advantage of every legitimate deduction without fear of future problems.

Investing is another powerful tool that can help you keep more money. In many countries, there are tax incentives for people who invest in their future, such as contributions to retirement funds or savings accounts for their children's education. These contributions not only help you prepare for the future, but they can also reduce your taxable income in the present. This means that in addition to saving, you're paying less tax, which is a double benefit.

If you're a freelancer or own a business, consider structuring your income in a way that optimizes your taxes. For example, instead of receiving all of your income as a salary, you could choose to set up a small business and pay yourself a lower salary, leaving the rest as business profits. Businesses often have access to tax deductions and benefits that aren't available to individuals, so this strategy can be very effective if implemented correctly. Of course, this requires planning and professional advice, but it can be a powerful way to keep more money.

Another strategy is to adjust your tax withholding. If you're an employee, you're probably familiar with the idea that your employer withholds a portion of your paycheck to pay taxes. However, many people allow too much to be withheld, resulting in a large refund at the end of the year. While receiving a large check can be exciting, in reality, what you're doing is loaning money to the government without charging interest. Adjusting your withholding to be more accurate means you'll have more money in your pocket each month, giving you greater financial flexibility throughout the year.

One topic you can't ignore is saving money in the long term through tax-smart investments. Some jurisdictions offer incentives for people who invest in certain sectors, such as green technology or research and development. If you have the resources to invest, these incentives not only allow your money to grow, but also help you reduce your tax burden. It's a strategy that requires a little more knowledge and, in some cases, professional advice, but it can be a very effective way to maximize your income.

Finally, don't forget the power of constantly educating yourself about the tax system. Laws change, and what works this year may not work next. Staying informed and aware of new tax opportunities is one way to ensure you're always getting the most out of the system. This may involve reading articles, taking basic finance courses, or simply spending time reviewing your options with a tax advisor.

Putting extra money in your pocket isn't a matter of luck or magic. It's the result of making informed decisions, planning ahead, and taking advantage of the opportunities the tax system offers you. When you take the time to understand how taxes work and apply smart strategies, you not only meet your legal obligations, but you also give yourself the opportunity to build a more stable and successful financial life. Because at the end of the day, every penny counts, and every strategy you use brings you a little closer to your financial goals.

Smart Tax Planning

Smart tax planning is not a concept reserved for big business owners or those with a team of financial advisors at their disposal. It is something that anyone can implement, regardless of their income, as long as they are willing to understand how taxes work and make strategic decisions throughout the year. It is like playing a game of chess: you need to know the rules, anticipate the moves and think ahead to maximize your resources and minimize the risks.

The essence of tax planning is simple: plan ahead. Many people make the mistake of leaving everything to the last minute, facing stress and pressure when tax time comes. Not only does this increase the chances of making mistakes, but it also limits your ability to take advantage of deductions, credits, and other tax opportunities. Good planning doesn't start in January or end in April. It's an ongoing effort that takes place throughout the year, tailored to your circumstances and financial goals.

The first step to smart tax planning is understanding your current situation. This includes knowing your income, your expenses, and how your taxes are calculated. If you work for a company, it is essential to know how much is being withheld from your salary and whether that amount is enough to cover your annual tax liability. If you are self-employed or run a business, you need to keep detailed records of all your income and expenses, as this will be the basis for determining how much you need to pay. Without this clarity, any attempt at planning will be like walking blind.

A key tool in tax planning is a budget. Although many people see it as boring or unnecessary, a good budget allows you to identify areas where you can save and adjust your spending to maximize your tax benefits. For example, if you know that certain purchases or investments are tax deductible, you can prioritize them in your budget and make sure to make these transactions before the tax year ends. Not only does this help you meet your financial goals, but it also reduces the amount of taxable income you will report.

Another essential part of tax planning is identifying the tax deductions and credits that are available to you. This isn't something you should leave to chance or assume your accountant will do it for you. Spend time researching what common deductions are for your situation, such as medical expenses, charitable donations, mortgage interest, or costs related to your job. If you own a business, the opportunities are even greater, as you can deduct everything from your office rent to marketing costs and business travel. Be sure to keep all necessary receipts and documents to support your deductions.

Tax credits are also worth your attention, as they have a direct impact on the amount of tax you have to pay. Some credits, such as those related to education, children, or investments in renewable energy, can make a big difference in your tax bill. However, many of these benefits have specific requirements, so it's important to understand them and make sure you meet them before you try to claim them.

If you own a business or are considering starting one, structuring your income and expenses strategically can be one of the most effective ways to reduce your tax burden. For example, you could push certain expenses to the end of the tax year to increase your deductions or defer income to the following year to spread your tax burden over time. These strategies require planning and, in some cases, professional advice, but can be very effective if executed correctly.

Another powerful strategy in tax planning is investing in your future. Contributions to retirement savings accounts, pension plans, or education savings accounts not only help you achieve your long-term goals, but they can also offer immediate tax benefits. In many cases, these contributions are tax-deductible, meaning you are saving for the future while reducing your current tax obligations. Plus, many governments offer additional incentives to encourage these investments, further increasing the benefit.

An often overlooked aspect of tax planning is the impact of investments. If you own stocks, real estate, or other assets, you need to understand how gains and losses from these investments affect your tax situation. In some cases, you can use losses from your investments to offset gains and reduce your taxable income. This is a more technical field, but with a little research or the help of a financial advisor, you can incorporate this strategy into your tax plan.

Insurance can also play an important role in tax planning. Some policies, such as savings life insurance or health plans, offer tax benefits that could help you reduce your taxes while protecting your family or assets. While these products may not be for everyone, they are worth considering as part of your overall strategy.

The key to making all this work is organization. It's not enough to have good intentions; you need a system to keep track of your income, expenses, deductions and credits. This can be as simple as using a spreadsheet or as advanced as specialized software. The important thing is that you have quick and easy access to all the information you need, especially when it comes time to file your taxes.

Last but not least, don't underestimate the value of having a trusted tax advisor or accountant. While you can learn a lot about the tax system on your own, a professional can help you identify opportunities you may not have considered and ensure you're complying with all regulations. This support is especially valuable if your finances are complex or you're looking to implement more advanced strategies.

Smart tax planning is not a luxury or a mystery reserved for a select few. It is a practice that anyone can adopt to take control of their finances, reduce their tax burden, and maximize their resources. With a little effort and dedication, you can turn what once seemed like an intimidating system into a tool that works in your favor. Because, at the end of the day, tax planning is not just about paying less taxes; it is about using the money you earn more intelligently and strategically to build the future you want.

How to Choose the Right Structure

Choosing the right structure for your business is one of the most important decisions you will make, not only because it defines how your company will operate, but also because it has a direct impact on your taxes, your legal responsibilities, and the way you manage your income. While this topic may seem complicated at first, the truth is that, with a little clarity and knowledge, you can find the option that best suits your needs and goals. The secret is to analyze your current circumstances, your future plans, and, above all, to understand how each structure affects your financial life.

When you decide to start a business, one of the first questions that arises is what type of legal structure you should choose. Options vary depending on the country, but generally include sole proprietorship, limited liability company, corporation, or cooperative, among others. Each of these structures has its own rules, advantages, and disadvantages, so there is no universal answer. The key is to choose the one that best aligns with your goals.

The simplest and most common option is to operate as a sole proprietor, also known as a freelancer in some countries. This model is ideal if you are starting out alone, with no partners or employees, and are looking to keep things simple. As a sole proprietor, you do not need to create a separate legal entity, meaning that you and your business are considered the same entity for tax and legal purposes. This makes things much simpler, but it also means that you are personally responsible for all of your business's debts and obligations. In terms of taxes, your business income is added directly to your personal return, which can be beneficial if your initial profits are modest, but can become costly as you grow as you may end up paying higher rates.

If you plan to work with partners or need to limit your personal liability, you might consider forming a limited liability company. This model is popular because it separates your personal finances from those of the business, meaning that in most cases you won't be personally liable for the company's debts. This protects your personal assets, such as your home or savings, should the business encounter financial problems. Additionally, a limited liability company can offer tax advantages, as in some cases it allows profits to be distributed more efficiently among partners, thereby optimizing the overall tax burden.

Another interesting option, especially if you plan to scale your business and attract investors, is to form a corporation. This model creates an entity completely separate from its owners, meaning the business can issue stock, hire employees, and make decisions independently. Tax-wise, corporations are typically subject to corporate taxes, which can be an advantage or disadvantage depending on the applicable tax rates and how you choose to distribute profits. For example, if you decide to reinvest profits instead of paying them out as dividends, you could significantly reduce your tax burden. However, corporations also come with more paperwork and administrative costs, so they aren't always the best option for small or early-stage businesses.

In some cases, especially if your business has a social or community purpose, you might consider forming a cooperative. This model is designed to benefit all of its members rather than maximizing profits. Cooperatives often receive tax benefits in many countries, but they have stricter rules about how profits are distributed and how decisions are made. This model can be ideal if you are working on a collaborative project with people who share your values and goals.

In addition to the structures mentioned above, there are also hybrids and variations that combine features of several models. For example, in some countries you can form a sole proprietorship with limited liability, which offers the simplicity of being self-employed but with the legal protection of a limited liability company. These types of options are great for entrepreneurs looking for a balance between simplicity and protection.

Regardless of the structure you choose, there are some key questions you should ask yourself in order to make an informed decision. What level of personal responsibility are you willing to take on? How big do you plan for your business to be in the next five or ten years? How do you want to handle taxes? Do you plan to work alone or with partners? Will you have employees? All of these questions will help you identify which structure best aligns with your needs and aspirations.

It's also important to consider the initial costs and time it will take to set up the structure you choose. Some options, such as operating as a sole proprietor, are very quick and inexpensive to set up. Others, such as a limited company, require more legal paperwork, registration costs, and a higher level of administrative maintenance. While these costs may seem like a hurdle at first, it's crucial to think long-term. Sometimes, spending a little more up front can save you a lot of money and trouble down the road.

Finally, never underestimate the value of professional advice. An experienced attorney or accountant can help you evaluate your options and ensure you fully understand the tax and legal implications of each structure. While hiring a professional may seem like an added expense, it's actually an investment that will help you avoid costly mistakes and streamline your operations from the start.

Choosing the right structure isn't just a matter of complying with legal regulations; it's a strategy that can help you maximize your income, reduce your taxes, and protect your assets. By taking the time to analyze your options and make an informed decision, you're building a solid foundation for your business' success — not just in the present, but in the future as well. Because, at the end of the day, the right structure isn't just a set of legal documents; it's a powerful tool that can make the difference between a business that's barely surviving and one that's thriving.

The Consequences of Tax Evasion

Tax evasion may seem, to some people, like a quick and easy way to save money. They may think that the government won't notice a missed bill or unreported income, or that even if they do, the consequences will be minimal. However, this perception couldn't be further from the truth. Not only is tax evasion illegal, but it can also trigger a number of serious consequences that affect both personally and professionally. The worst part is that many of these consequences don't just involve financial penalties, they can also ruin your reputation and future prospects.

First, let's talk about penalties. Most countries' tax systems have very strict policies against tax evasion, and one of the first consequences you'll face if you're caught is a significant fine. These fines aren't small; in many cases, they can be a significant percentage of the unreported amount, plus accrued interest for the time that has passed since you should have paid. Even if you manage to correct your mistake and pay the back taxes, the interest and penalties can push the total to a figure that exceeds your initial calculations. Not only can this throw your finances out of balance, but it can also put your personal assets at risk if you don't have the resources to pay.

In addition to fines, there is the risk of facing criminal charges. In some cases, tax evasion is not simply about mistakes or carelessness, but about deliberate acts to hide income or report false information. When tax authorities detect that a person or company is acting intentionally to avoid their obligations, they can initiate legal proceedings that include criminal charges. This means that you could face not only fines and seizures, but also a possible prison sentence. Imagine the impact this would have on your life: from losing your freedom to damaging your professional and personal reputation in a way that could be difficult to repair.

Loss of trust is another devastating consequence of tax evasion. If you run a business, your clients, partners, and investors expect you to operate with integrity. Once your name is associated with tax evasion, that level of trust can disappear in an instant. People prefer to work with companies and individuals who comply with their obligations, and such an accusation can result in you losing important contracts, being left without financial support, and even facing boycotts. In the business world, trust is everything, and a stain on your record can haunt you for years.

Another consequence that is often overlooked is the emotional and psychological impact. Living in constant fear of being discovered by the tax authorities can be exhausting. This stress can affect your quality of life, your mental health, and even your personal relationships. People who have evaded taxes often describe the experience as living with a dark cloud hanging over their heads, always waiting for the moment when someone will knock on their door to confront them. This level of anxiety is not worth any temporary savings you think you have made.

There is also the issue of garnishments and audits. When the government discovers that you have not paid your taxes, they have the right to take drastic measures to recover what you owe them. This can include seizing your bank account, seizing personal property, or even putting property up for auction to cover the amount owed. Furthermore, being detected as a tax evader can lead to the authorities placing you under constant scrutiny, subjecting you to frequent audits that will see every aspect of your finances scrutinized. Not only is this time-consuming, but it also creates a level of invasion of your privacy that few people are willing to tolerate.

For businesses, tax evasion can be even more disastrous. In addition to fines and penalties, a business caught evading taxes could face having its operating license revoked or being shut down for good. This means that not only could you lose your source of income, but employees who rely on your business could also be put out of work. Tax evasion is not a victimless crime; it affects an entire network of people who rely on the stability of your operations.

At a societal level, tax evasion has an even greater impact. When individuals or businesses do not pay their fair share, the tax burden is redistributed among those who do comply with their obligations. This means that your neighbors, your colleagues, and future generations end up paying for the shortcomings caused by evasion. In addition, the lack of tax revenue affects the government's ability to fund essential services such as education, health, infrastructure, and security. When you choose not to pay taxes, you are contributing to a less equitable system and leaving others to shoulder a responsibility that is also yours.

One of the most common excuses people use to justify tax avoidance is that they believe taxes are unfair or that money is not being spent properly. While it is true that there is always room for improvement in how public resources are managed, this does not justify evasion. There are legal channels to challenge and improve the tax system, from getting involved in political initiatives to advocating for reforms. But evading taxes is not only illegal, it also perpetuates the problems you are trying to avoid.

The good news is that there are always legal ways to optimize your taxes and reduce your tax burden without falling into evasion. From taking advantage of tax deductions and credits to structuring your income strategically, there are many ways to comply with your obligations and, at the same time, keep more money in your pocket. The key is to be proactive, stay informed and seek professional advice when necessary.

Evading taxes may seem like an easy solution in the short term, but the consequences are serious and long-lasting. Not only do you risk facing fines, seizures, and criminal penalties, but you can also lose your reputation, your financial stability, and even your peace of mind. At the end of the day, paying taxes is not only a legal obligation, but also a social responsibility that benefits us all. Accepting this reality and acting with integrity will not only keep you out of trouble, but will also allow you to build a stronger, worry-free future.

How to Recognize an Illegal Scheme

Illegal tax evasion schemes have been around since governments began collecting money, and while laws have evolved over time to detect and punish them, there are still those who try to take advantage of legal loopholes or deceive authorities to avoid paying what they owe. The dangerous thing about these schemes is that they are often presented as legitimate financial strategies, with promises of large tax savings and no apparent consequences. But the reality is very different. Anyone who falls for an illegal scheme can end up facing fines, criminal penalties, and even prison. Therefore, knowing how to recognize them is essential to avoid legal problems and protect your assets.

A clear indicator that you are dealing with an illegal scheme is when someone promises you that you can eliminate your taxes completely. It is true that there are legal strategies to reduce your tax burden, but none allow you to stop paying taxes completely. If someone tells you that they can do this, you should be immediately suspicious. Taxes are an obligation established by law, and any method that seeks to eliminate them entirely almost always involves falsifying documents, hiding income or manipulating accounting, all of which are illegal practices.

Another red flag is when an advisor or company offers to take part in a scheme that seems too good to be true. Often, these schemes involve moving money through multiple accounts, shell companies, or even offshore accounts with the promise that they will be invisible to the government. The reality is that governments increasingly have more tools to track financial movements, especially with international agreements that allow for the sharing of banking information between countries. If someone tells you that you can hide income by simply depositing it in an account outside the country, you are very likely entering into a fraudulent scheme.

You should also be wary of any scheme that involves the use of fake invoices. This is one of the most common methods used by those trying to evade taxes, and although it may seem like a harmless practice, tax authorities have developed increasingly sophisticated systems to detect them. A fake invoice is one that documents a transaction that never occurred, usually with the purpose of inflating expenses and reducing taxes payable. If a company or person offers you these types of invoices to reduce your tax burden, the best thing you can do is walk away immediately, because participating in this type of fraud can bring severe consequences, including criminal charges.

Another illegal scheme you should learn to recognize is the use of shell companies or fictitious companies. These companies are created for the sole purpose of simulating operations and fraudulently moving money. On the outside, they may look like legitimate businesses, but in reality they have no employees, real customers, or genuine operations. Their only function is to divert income, generate fake invoices, or hide assets. If you are ever offered to be part of a company that has no real activity but promises to help you reduce taxes, you should know that you are dealing with a fraudulent scheme.

Some of the most sophisticated illegal schemes involve the use of trusts or complex corporate structures to conceal the true ownership of income or assets. While trusts and business structures can be legitimate financial planning tools, some promoters use them to create a false separation between the taxpayer and his or her assets, with the intent of avoiding paying taxes. In most cases, tax authorities can trace these structures and prove that the income actually still belongs to the original taxpayer, which can result in serious penalties.

Another illegal scheme to avoid is tax withholding manipulation. Some companies, in an attempt to cut costs, withhold taxes from their employees or suppliers but never turn them over to the government. Not only is this illegal, but it can also lead to serious financial problems for those who rely on those payments for future benefits or to avoid tax problems of their own. If you work for a company that does this, you could be affected without even realizing it, and if you're a business owner, falling into this practice can land you in serious legal trouble.

Using false identities or nominees is another clear sign of an illegal scheme. Sometimes, evaders use family members, friends or even fictitious people to open bank accounts, register property or receive income in their name, hoping that this will make them invisible to tax authorities. But monitoring systems are becoming more sophisticated and can detect suspicious patterns. Even if you think no one will notice, chances are that sooner or later you will be caught.

Another red flag is when you are told you can report less income than you actually earned. Some promoters of fraudulent schemes argue that tax authorities cannot track all income and that it is safe to declare less than you actually earned. However, governments have multiple tools to identify discrepancies between what you declare and what you actually earn. From cross-checking bank information to accessing supplier and customer records, authorities can detect if your reported income does not match reality.

If you are ever offered a strategy that requires you to hide information, omit data on your return, or manipulate records, it is a clear sign that you are dealing with an illegal scheme. The best way to avoid falling into these traps is to maintain a policy of complete transparency in your tax returns. If a strategy cannot be explained clearly and simply, without the need to hide anything, it is probably not legitimate.

It is crucial to remember that the consequences of participating in illegal schemes not only affect your wallet, but can put your freedom, reputation and long-term financial stability at risk. In many countries, tax crimes carry prison sentences, in addition to financial penalties and damage to your credit and business history.

The best way to protect yourself is to always seek advice from trusted professionals. A good accountant or tax lawyer will never suggest a strategy that involves hiding information or manipulating figures. If at any time you feel that you are being offered something suspicious, consult another professional before making a decision. In tax matters, cheap can be extremely expensive.

Recognizing an illegal scheme not only protects you from legal problems, but also allows you to build a solid financial future based on transparency and security. Taxes can be a complicated topic, but there are many legal ways to optimize them without risking falling into fraudulent practices. The key is to be informed, be cautious and always act with integrity.

Why Honesty is Profitable

Many people see paying taxes as an unnecessary sacrifice, an obligation that takes away money that could be spent on other things. Some even believe that finding a way to pay less, even through questionable methods, is a sign of financial savvy. But what is not always understood is that honesty, in fiscal and financial terms, is not only a moral duty, but also a profitable strategy. Being transparent with taxes and handling finances ethically has benefits that go far beyond avoiding legal problems. In fact, it can become a competitive advantage that will allow you to grow in a stable and secure way.

One of the biggest benefits of honesty is peace of mind. There is nothing more stressful than living in constant fear that at any moment you could be hit with an audit, a penalty, or even a legal charge for tax evasion. Those who try to cheat the system may enjoy momentary relief by paying less tax, but that savings becomes a psychological burden when the risk of being discovered is ever present. On the other hand, when you manage your finances clearly and comply with your tax obligations, you can focus on growing your business or your income without the shadow of a possible investigation.

From a financial perspective, being honest about taxes and finances opens many doors. Banks, investors, and business partners prefer to work with people and companies that have a clean and transparent track record. If you need a loan to expand your business, a mortgage to buy a property, or an investor who trusts your project, the first thing they will look at is your tax and financial history. If you have been hiding income or manipulating your statements, you will most likely not be able to prove financial stability, which will drastically reduce your opportunities. On the other hand, if you have managed your finances in an orderly and honest manner, you will have an easier time accessing credit and financing under better conditions.

Another important aspect is reputation. In the world of business and finance, trust is everything. Customers, suppliers and partners want to do business with people who are trustworthy and do not represent a risk. If your name or that of your company is caught up in a scandal for tax evasion or fraud, the trust you have built over the years can crumble in an instant. Recovering from a reputational blow can be extremely difficult and, in many cases, impossible. Instead, being recognized as a person or company that fulfills its obligations and acts with integrity will allow you to build long-lasting and beneficial business relationships.

Honesty also protects you from unsustainable growth. Some companies or individuals who seek to evade taxes and manipulate their finances do so to give the appearance of financial strength that is not real. These types of practices can lead to wrong decisions, such as taking on debts they cannot pay or investing in projects without solid financial backing. Over time, these decisions end up generating bigger problems and, in many cases, bankruptcy. When you manage your finances honestly, you know exactly how much money you have, how much you can invest, and what the real state of your economy is. This allows you to make informed decisions and build stable and sustainable growth.

From a legal standpoint, complying with taxes and managing your finances correctly can prevent problems that can turn into nightmares. Many people believe that tax evasion is just an administrative problem, but in reality, in many countries it is a serious crime that can lead to prison sentences, seizure of assets and penalties that can wipe out a person or company's assets. What at first seems like simple savings can end up costing much more in fines, lawyers and legal problems. On the other hand, those who comply with their tax obligations can sleep peacefully, knowing that they will not face legal problems that could put their future at risk.

Honesty also fosters a culture of discipline and organization. Managing finances correctly requires planning, order, and strategy, qualities that are essential for success in any area. When you keep proper control of your income and expenses, you better understand how your money works and can find ways to optimize it without resorting to illegal practices. People and companies that have good financial habits manage to generate more wealth in the long term because they have real control over their resources and can make better decisions.

Another benefit of honesty is that it allows you to take advantage of legitimate tax opportunities. Many times, those who try to evade taxes illegally are unaware that there are completely legal tax deductions, incentives and strategies that can reduce the tax burden without having to take risks. There are legal ways to optimize taxes, from deductions for investments to benefits for social contributions. But to access these opportunities, it is necessary to be within the legal framework and have clear and orderly accounting.

At a societal level, being honest with taxes also contributes to collective well-being. Taxes fund essential services such as health, education, security and infrastructure – things that we all use and need. While we may not always agree with how governments manage resources, tax evasion only makes the problem worse. When some people do not pay their fair share, the burden is redistributed to those who do, creating a more unfair system. On the other hand, when everyone contributes fairly, resources can be managed better and improvements in the quality of life of the whole society can be achieved.

Ultimately, honesty is an investment in the future. Building a career, business or wealth on solid and transparent foundations ensures that growth is sustainable and that there are no unpleasant surprises along the way. Many of the most successful people and companies in the world have understood that transparency and integrity are not obstacles to success, but rather tools that allow it to be achieved with greater security and stability. Being honest does not mean paying more than necessary, but rather paying what is fair and finding legitimate ways to optimize resources without falling into unnecessary risks.

Honesty pays off because it protects your peace of mind, strengthens your reputation, allows you to access financial opportunities, avoids legal problems and fosters a culture of discipline and organization that generates real growth. Although it may sometimes seem that those who look for shortcuts have an advantage, the reality is that in the long term, those who build their success on honest and transparent foundations are the ones who achieve true success and the financial stability that everyone seeks.

Investing with Tax Intelligence

Investing is one of the best ways to grow your money, but doing so without considering the tax impact can mean losing a significant portion of your earnings to taxes. Many people focus solely on choosing profitable investments without thinking about how taxes will affect their returns. Tax intelligence is not about avoiding taxes, but about strategically structuring your investments to maximize profits and reduce the tax burden within the legal framework. Understanding how taxes work for each type of investment can make the difference between building wealth efficiently or seeing a significant portion of your earnings disappear in unnecessary payments to the tax authorities.

One of the first things to consider is what type of tax affects each investment. Not all investments are taxed the same, and knowing the difference between ordinary income, capital gains, and passive income can help you make better decisions. For example, income from wages or businesses is typically subject to higher taxes than capital gains generated by the sale of assets such as stocks or real estate. In many countries, taxes on long-term capital gains are significantly lower than taxes on regular income. This means that if you hold an investment longer instead of selling it quickly, you could reduce what you pay in taxes and increase your net return.

Another key point in tax-smart investing is taking advantage of accounts or structures that offer tax advantages. Many governments encourage saving and investing by offering special accounts that allow you to defer or even eliminate taxes on certain earnings. In some countries, there are tax-advantaged retirement accounts where contributions can be tax-deductible and earnings can grow without being taxed until retirement. There are also tax-free investment accounts, where the returns obtained do not generate any tax burden if certain requirements are met. Using these types of tools allows your money to grow faster by preventing a portion of your earnings from being lost to taxes each year.

Real estate also offers multiple tax advantages that many investors are unaware of. In many countries, purchasing real estate can provide tax benefits such as deductions for depreciation, operating expenses, and maintenance costs. Depreciation is a powerful tool because it allows you to reduce your tax burden by reporting an accounting loss on the value of the property, even when the property is actually appreciating. Additionally, if you use financing to purchase a property, the mortgage interest may be tax deductible, further reducing the amount of tax you pay on your rental income. With good planning, real estate can become a highly profitable investment with minimal tax burden.

Investments in companies can also benefit from smart tax strategies. If you own a business or are involved as an investor in a company, structuring your stake appropriately can legally reduce your tax burden. For example, instead of receiving all of your income in the form of a salary, you could structure part of your profits as dividends, which in many cases have more favorable tax treatment. There are also tax incentives for reinvesting profits, meaning that instead of taking all of the money out, you can reinvest it back into the business and reduce the amount of tax you pay. In some countries, there are even tax benefits for investing in startups or technology companies, where investors can access tax credits or tax breaks.

Diversification is another key strategy for tax-smart investing. It's not just about reducing financial risks, but also about optimizing your tax burden. By diversifying across different types of assets with different tax treatments, you can balance your income so that you pay less tax in the long term. For example, combining real estate investments with stocks, bonds, and index funds can help you access different tax benefits and take advantage of lower tax periods for each type of asset. A common mistake is to concentrate all your capital in a single source of income that is highly taxed, which can mean missing out on tax optimization opportunities.

When you decide to sell an investment also influences how much tax you'll pay. Many people sell assets without considering the tax implications of the timing. If you sell an investment in a year when you already have a high income, you could end up paying more taxes than if you sold it in a year when your tax burden is lower. Some strategies allow you to defer taxes through asset exchanges or planned sales, which helps minimize your tax burden over time. There are also tax-loss harvesting strategies, which involve selling investments that have lost value to offset taxes on gains from other investments, thereby reducing your overall tax burden.

Investment funds and collective investment companies can also offer tax advantages if chosen correctly. In many cases, efficiently structured funds can distribute profits with a lower tax burden or allow investors to defer taxes until withdrawal. In addition, some specialized funds invest in sectors that have tax incentives, such as renewable energy, technology or infrastructure, which can provide additional tax benefits.

Tax planning for investments is not just about paying less tax, but about maximizing the net return on your investments. The difference between an investor who pays taxes efficiently and one who does not can be huge over the years. If two people invest the same amount of money and get the same return, but one of them pays less tax thanks to proper planning, that person will end up with significantly more wealth in the long run.

To invest tax-wise, it is essential to stay informed about the tax laws and regulations in force in your country. Rules change over time, and what works today might not be the best strategy in the future. Having a good financial advisor or an accountant specialized in investments can make a big difference and help you take advantage of all legal opportunities to reduce taxes and maximize profits.

Ultimately, tax-smart investing doesn't mean looking for illegal shortcuts or hiding money, but rather using the tools and strategies available within the legal framework to ensure that your investments grow as efficiently as possible. The key is to structure your investments in a way that takes advantage of legitimate tax benefits, properly diversify your portfolio, and plan each move considering its short- and long-term tax impact. Doing this will not only allow you to pay less tax legally, but it will also help you build wealth sustainably and with less risk.

The Art of Billing Correctly

Invoicing correctly is much more than issuing a simple document. It is a fundamental part of any business, large or small, and doing it well can make the difference between paying the right taxes or ending up with financial problems, penalties and unexpected audits. Many people see invoicing as a boring or unnecessary procedure, but in reality it is a key tool for organizing finances, maintaining a healthy business and avoiding conflicts with tax authorities. Mastering the art of invoicing correctly will not only allow you to comply with the law, but will also help you optimize your tax burden and strengthen the credibility of your business.

One of the most common mistakes entrepreneurs and business owners make is not giving importance to invoicing from the start of their activities. Some people believe that they can postpone this aspect until their business grows, while others choose to operate informally to avoid paying taxes. However, this mentality can become a major obstacle in the long run. Not issuing invoices means that you cannot legally prove your income, which will prevent you from accessing bank loans, applying for financing or even participating in contracts with larger companies that require proper tax documentation. In addition, working without invoicing can lead to serious legal problems if the tax authorities detect undeclared income.

Each country has its own rules and regulations regarding invoicing, but there are basic principles that apply in almost all tax systems. An invoice must contain accurate and complete information about the transaction. This includes the details of the issuer and the recipient, a detailed description of the goods or services provided, the total amount, applicable taxes, and the method of payment. Often, through carelessness or ignorance, people leave out key information or make mistakes when issuing invoices, which can lead to rejections, audits, or even fines. Reviewing each invoice before issuing it is a simple but effective practice to avoid problems.

Another key point in invoicing is to ensure that invoices are correctly recorded in the business's accounting. Issuing invoices without proper control can generate inconsistencies in financial records, which can lead to problems with tax payments. A good practice is to have a digital invoicing system or use accounting software that automates the process and reduces human errors. Currently, in many countries it is mandatory to use electronic invoicing, which facilitates tax control and allows for better management of financial information.

One aspect that many business owners are unaware of is that invoicing also has a direct impact on their tax burden. Issuing invoices correctly allows you to access tax deductions and avoid unnecessary tax payments. In many tax systems, certain expenses may be deductible if they are supported by valid invoices. This means that if you buy supplies, equipment or hire services for your business, it is essential to request invoices that include all the correct tax information in order to record them as deductible expenses. Not requesting invoices for your expenses can result in paying more taxes than you really should.

Another common invoicing mistake is the misuse of terms and descriptions. Many people issue invoices with vague or generic descriptions such as “services rendered” or “sales of products,” without specifying what the transaction is actually about. This can raise questions during an audit and, in some cases, can cause an invoice to be rejected as valid. It is important to be as detailed as possible when describing the goods or services invoiced, including quantities, units of measurement, and any other relevant information. A clear and detailed invoice not only facilitates tax control, but also instills confidence in customers and suppliers.

It is also important to be aware of the invoicing deadlines and requirements set by your country's tax authority. In many places, invoices must be issued within a certain time after the transaction, and there are specific rules on how they should be stored and presented in case of an inspection. Failing to meet these deadlines can lead to penalties and administrative problems that can affect the operation of your business. Having a control system over invoices issued and received is essential to avoid inconveniences.

The issue of false or apocryphal invoices is another aspect that deserves attention. In some sectors, it is common to find fraudulent practices where invoices are issued without real support to inflate expenses and reduce taxes. Although it may seem like a "smart" way to pay less taxes, participating in this type of scheme is extremely risky. Tax authorities have increasingly sophisticated systems to detect false invoices, and the consequences can range from high fines to criminal penalties. The best strategy will always be to stay within the legal framework and take advantage of legitimate tax tools to optimize the tax burden.

It's also important to consider how invoicing affects your relationship with your customers. In some cases, customers may request invoices with incorrect information or ask for changes to reduce their own tax burden. Accepting these types of practices can compromise the integrity of your business and expose you to legal problems in the future. It's essential to establish clear policies regarding issuing invoices and to ensure that all transactions are recorded correctly and transparently.

Finally, well-managed invoicing allows you to have a clearer view of the financial health of your business. Keeping proper control of invoices issued and received helps you analyze income, detect consumption patterns, evaluate profit margins and make strategic decisions based on real information. A business that invoices correctly not only complies with the law, but is also positioned to grow in an orderly and sustainable manner.

Mastering the art of proper invoicing not only protects you from tax problems, but also gives you access to benefits such as tax optimization, better financing opportunities, and greater credibility in the market. The key is to be meticulous, use technological tools that facilitate the process, and make sure that each transaction is recorded clearly and accurately. Proper invoicing is not just an obligation, it is a smart strategy to strengthen your business and ensure its long-term success.

A Powerful Couple

When it comes to money and taxes, there is one combination that can make the difference between someone who is financially stuck and someone who is smart about building wealth. That combination is well-managed money and a smart tax strategy. Together, they create a powerful pair that allows you to grow your wealth, minimize unnecessary losses, and take advantage of the opportunities the system offers. However, many people only care about making more money without understanding that, if they don't know how to manage it correctly, much of that income can end up in the hands of the tax authorities instead of working in their favor.

The problem is that most people view taxes as an inevitable punishment and not as a variable that can be strategically managed. They earn money, pay taxes and keep the remainder, not realizing that there are legal and effective ways to optimize that process to keep more. The key is to understand that income and taxes should not be treated separately, but as two elements that must work together to maximize results. This is where the importance of planning each financial decision with a tax perspective comes into play.

One of the most common mistakes people make is believing that financial success only depends on how much money they earn. There are people with high salaries who end up paying so much tax that they barely manage to accumulate wealth, while others, with more modest incomes, know how to structure their finances efficiently and manage to keep a larger proportion of what they generate. The difference is in tax planning. It is not about evading taxes, but about knowing and applying the rules of the system intelligently to pay only what is required, without losing money unnecessarily.

For this powerful couple to work, the first step is to be fully aware of the tax options available. There are multiple legal tools that allow you to reduce your tax burden, but many people don't even know they exist. For example, there are tax deductions that allow you to subtract certain expenses before calculating the taxes you owe, such as investments in education, health insurance, donations, business-related expenses, or even mortgage interest. There are also specific tax incentives for certain types of investments, such as retirement plans, real estate purchases, or business creation. Those who don't know about these options simply pay more taxes than they should.

Another key point is the legal structure in which income is generated. Earning money as an employee is not the same as earning money as an entrepreneur or investor. A salaried employee generally has fewer options for tax optimization, as taxes are deducted directly from his or her pay before the money reaches him or her hands. In contrast, an entrepreneur or self-employed professional has the possibility to organize his or her income more flexibly, deduct legitimate expenses, and pay taxes on a lower tax base. This means that it is not just how much you earn that matters, but how you earn it.

Choosing the type of legal entity under which you operate is also critical to this strategy. Many people start businesses as individuals without realizing that forming a company or corporation can offer them significant tax advantages. Depending on the country and the type of activity, tax rates may be lower for companies than for individuals, and some expenses can be deducted more effectively if handled through a business structure. Additionally, there are preferential tax regimes for certain sectors that can further reduce the tax burden.

Tax planning is not just about reducing taxes, but also about taking advantage of investment opportunities that maximize capital growth. A person who simply saves money in a bank account and lets taxes eat away at their purchasing power year after year is missing out on opportunities. In contrast, someone who uses tax strategies to invest in tax-advantaged assets, such as tax-deferred mutual funds or real estate with depreciation deductions, is able to grow their money more efficiently and with less tax impact.

Timing also plays a key role in this equation. Paying taxes immediately is not the same as strategically deferring them for the future.

There are mechanisms that allow you to postpone paying certain taxes until a time when the tax burden is lower. For example, in some countries, capital gains can be deferred by reinvesting them in certain assets, thus avoiding paying taxes until the time of final sale. The same is true for retirement plans, which allow you to reduce your tax base in the present and pay taxes only at the time of withdrawal, when the tax rate is generally lower.

Another important factor is income diversification. Not relying on just one source of income not only reduces financial risks, but also allows you to optimize your tax burden. Different types of income may be subject to different tax rates, and a person with multiple sources of income can organize their finances in a way that minimizes the amount of tax they pay. For example, a combination of salary income, passive rental income, stock dividends, and capital gains can offer a more efficient tax structure than relying solely on one salary.

In addition to income structure, good tax advice is essential. Many people make costly mistakes because they try to handle everything on their own without a thorough understanding of tax laws. A good accountant or financial advisor can help you identify tax-saving opportunities, avoid mistakes that can lead to penalties, and design a customized tax strategy based on your specific situation. The difference between someone who pays taxes without planning and someone who has a well-designed tax strategy can be huge over the years.

Ultimately, the key to financial success is not just about making more money, but knowing how to manage it with fiscal intelligence. Money and tax strategy are an inseparable pair that, when working in harmony, allow you to build wealth in a solid and sustainable way. It is not about juggling to pay less taxes at any cost, but about using the rules of the game in your favor in a completely legal and strategic way. With the right information and tools, anyone can improve their financial situation and ensure that every dollar earned is used in the best possible way.

Building wealth is not just a matter of effort and talent, but also of knowledge. The difference between someone who struggles their whole life to stay afloat and someone who achieves financial freedom often lies in how well they understand and apply the relationship between income and taxes. In the end, true wealth is not just about earning more, but learning to keep more of what you generate, and that is the true magic of this powerful couple.

Common Mistakes and How to Avoid Them

One of the biggest problems with taxes is not just paying them, but making mistakes that end up costing you more money, time, and headaches than necessary. Many people fall into common traps simply because they don't know how the tax system works or because they leave everything to the last minute without a clear strategy. Avoiding these mistakes will not only help you pay what is fair and necessary, but it will also allow you to better take advantage of tax opportunities that can leave more money in your pocket.

The first mistake most people make is not keeping proper track of their income and expenses. Many people think that taxes are only paid once a year and that they don't need to worry about it until the deadline comes. The problem with this mindset is that when it finally comes time to file, they find themselves in a financial mess where receipts are missing, they can't remember certain expenses, or worse, they've made mistakes during the year that they can't fix. Keeping an orderly record of your finances is key to making sure you don't pay more than you should and that you can take advantage of all the tax deductions and benefits available.

Another common mistake is not taking advantage of tax deductions. Many people pay more taxes than they should simply because they don't know which expenses can be deducted. For example, in some countries you can deduct medical expenses, education, donations, mortgage interest, contributions to retirement plans, and even some work-related expenses if you are self-employed or own a business. The problem is that many people don't keep the necessary receipts or don't find out which deductions apply to them. The solution is simple: get informed and organize your documents to make sure that every penny you can deduct is accounted for correctly.

It is also very common to make mistakes when choosing the legal structure to generate income. For example, many people work as freelancers without formalizing their business and end up paying taxes as if they were employees, which is often less tax efficient. Depending on the legislation of each country, having a registered company can offer benefits such as paying less taxes on certain income, deducting more expenses or accessing special tax regimes. Evaluating the best structure for your situation is essential to optimize what you pay and avoid losing money unnecessarily.

Another common problem is mixing personal and business finances. Many small business owners and freelancers make the mistake of using just one bank account for everything, which makes it difficult to control expenses and can lead to missing out on important deductions. In addition, this lack of separation can lead to problems with the tax authority in the event of an audit, as it becomes difficult to prove which expenses are really related to the economic activity and which are personal. The best solution is always to keep separate accounts and be disciplined with money management.

Failing to plan tax payments in advance is another mistake that can lead to serious financial problems. Many people wait until the last minute to figure out how much they need to pay and then find themselves with an unpleasant surprise: a higher-than-expected tax bill. In some cases, this leads to people not having enough money to pay on time, leading to interest, penalties, and legal problems. To avoid this, it is best to make regular estimates of what needs to be paid and set aside that money in advance. Having a strategy for advance payments or partial payments during the year can make the tax burden more manageable and avoid last-minute scares.

One mistake that many people underestimate is not correctly declaring all their income. Some people think that they can omit certain income without consequences, but the reality is that the tax authority has multiple mechanisms to track the money you receive. From information provided by banks and employers to cross-checking data with other institutions, it is increasingly difficult to hide income. If the authority detects discrepancies, you can face audits, fines or even more serious legal problems. The best strategy is always to correctly declare everything you earn and make sure that your tax information is consistent with reality.

Another dangerous mistake is blindly trusting a tax advisor without understanding what they are doing. Many people completely delegate the handling of their taxes to an accountant without bothering to review what is being declared. This can be a problem if the advisor makes a mistake or applies questionable strategies that can get you into trouble with the tax authority. Although having a good advisor is key to optimizing your tax burden, you should always have a basic understanding of what is being done with your money. Ask questions, review the documents before signing, and make sure everything is in order.

Failing to stay up to date on tax changes is also a mistake that can cost you dearly. Tax laws are constantly changing, and what worked last year may not work this year. New deductions may become available, certain tax rates may change, or new regulations may affect your situation. Failing to stay informed can cause you to miss out on tax opportunities or, worse yet, make unintentional mistakes that result in penalties. The solution is simple: take the time to review tax news, consult with an expert, or use reliable sources to stay up to date.

One mistake that many people make is not diversifying their income to optimize their tax burden. Not all income is taxed equally, and some sources may have more favorable tax rates than others. For example, in some countries investment income is taxed at a lower rate than wages, or certain types of businesses may have access to tax benefits that do not apply to others. Not diversifying and relying on a single source of income can result in you paying more taxes than necessary, while a well-structured strategy can help you legally reduce your tax burden.

Finally, one of the biggest mistakes people make is viewing taxes as a punishment rather than a normal part of financial life. This mindset causes many people to make impulsive decisions, seek out dubious schemes to pay less, or simply ignore their tax obligations until it is too late. Taxes do not have to be an unbearable burden if they are handled with intelligence and planning. Instead of seeing them as an obstacle, it is better to treat them as part of a financial strategy that, when well managed, can help you build wealth and security in the long term.

Avoiding these mistakes will not only help you pay less tax legally, but it will also give you financial peace of mind. With organization, planning, and knowledge, anyone can optimize their tax burden and make sure their money is used in the best possible way. Taxes don't have to be a problem if you know how to handle them correctly.

The Path to Financial and Tax Freedom

Financial and fiscal freedom is not a concept exclusive to millionaires or economic experts. It is an achievable goal for anyone who is willing to organize their finances, learn about taxes, and apply smart strategies to make their money work for them. The problem is that most people see taxes as an enemy, instead of understanding that, well managed, they can be a tool to generate wealth and stability in the long term.

The first step to achieving financial and fiscal freedom is knowing exactly how much you earn and how much you spend. It may seem basic, but most people don't have a clear idea of their own finances. They spend without control, pay taxes without checking if they are paying more than necessary, and are unaware of what tax benefits they could be taking advantage of. Before thinking about advanced strategies, you need to know exactly where your money is going each month. Keeping a detailed record of income and expenses will allow you to make informed decisions and avoid unpleasant surprises.

Once you have clarity about your finances, the next step is to legally reduce the impact of taxes on your income. This is where tax planning comes into play. It's not about evading taxes or making questionable maneuvers, but rather using the rules to your advantage. There are multiple strategies to pay less taxes in a completely legal way, such as taking advantage of tax deductions, choosing the right structure to generate income, investing in tax-advantaged financial vehicles, and strategically distributing income. Each country has different opportunities, but the key point is to research and apply the ones that best suit your situation.

Another key aspect is understanding how different types of income work. Not all the money you earn is taxed the same, and some sources of income are taxed much lower than others. For example, in many countries passive income, such as income from investments or property rentals, has more favorable tax rates than salary income. If you only rely on a traditional job, you are likely paying one of the highest tax rates. Diversifying your sources of income is one of the most effective ways to optimize your tax burden and get closer to financial freedom.

The next step is to maximize your savings and investments with tax intelligence. Many people invest their money without considering the tax impact, which can significantly reduce their returns. For example, if you invest in assets that generate highly taxed income, you could be losing a significant portion of your earnings in taxes. However, if you choose tax-advantaged investment vehicles, such as tax-advantaged retirement accounts or reinvestment strategies that defer tax payments, you can grow your money much faster. The key is to not only invest, but to do so with a tax-efficient approach.

One strategy that many people overlook is the use of legal structures to optimize taxes. Depending on the laws of each country, it may be more convenient to operate through a company, a partnership, or even a foundation rather than receiving all income as an individual. These types of structures can offer benefits such as lower tax rates, access to additional deductions, and greater flexibility in money management. These are not gimmicks or aggressive schemes, but rather choosing the best legal way to manage your income to pay only what is fair and necessary.

Long-term tax planning is another key element on the path to financial freedom. It's not enough to think about how to cut taxes this year; you need a sustainable strategy that works throughout your entire financial life. For example, if you save for retirement in a tax-efficient way, you can accumulate much more money than if you simply saved without considering taxes. Similarly, if you plan for the passing on of your wealth with proper tax strategies, you can prevent a large portion of your money from ending up in the hands of the government instead of your heirs.

Another essential point is to avoid costly mistakes in tax administration. Many people lose money because they do not file their returns correctly, forget deductions or make mistakes that result in fines and penalties. A tax audit can become a nightmare if you have not kept good control of your finances.

The best way to avoid these problems is to be proactive, keep organized records and, if necessary, have the support of a reliable tax advisor.

Ultimately, true financial freedom isn't just about making more money or paying less taxes, it's about having complete control over your finances. Many people, even with high incomes, live with financial stress because they spend more than they earn, have poorly managed debts, or simply don't understand how money works. The key is to build a mindset of planning, control, and ongoing financial education.

The path to financial and tax freedom isn't an overnight process, but every smart decision you make today brings you one step closer. The difference between those who achieve financial independence and those who are forever stuck in money trouble isn't how much income they make, but how they manage that income. By learning how to strategically manage taxes and make your money work for you, you can enjoy a life with fewer financial worries and more opportunities for growth.

www.ingramcontent.com/pod-product-compliance
Lightning Source LLC
LaVergne TN
LVHW090421210926
848480LV00002B/638
* 9 7 9 8 2 2 7 8 4 3 4 6 3 *